# His thoughts said . . .
# His Father said . . .

Amidst the multitude of thoughts
   Which in my heart do fight,
My soul, lest it be overcharg'd,
   Thy comforts do delight.

Those that are broken in their heart,
   And grievèd in their minds,
He healeth, and their painful wounds
   He tenderly up-binds.

Ps. 94. 19.  Ps. 174. 3.
Scots metrical version.

# His thoughts said . . .
# His Father said . . .

### Dohnavur Fellowship

**And every thought of holiness
is His alone**

## CHRISTIAN LITERATURE CRUSADE
### FORT WASHINGTON   PENNSYLVANIA

# CHRISTIAN LITERATURE CRUSADE

### CANADA
1440 Mackay Street, Montreal, Quebec

### GREAT BRITAIN
39 Ludgate Hill, London E.C.4

### AUSTRALIA
Eastwood, Sydney, New South Wales

### NEW ZEALAND
Box 1688, Auckland, C.1

*Also in:* Europe—South America—Africa
Caribbean Area—India—Indonesia
Philippines—Pakistan—Japan
Korea—Thailand—New Guinea

MADE IN GREAT BRITAIN

*About this little book :—*

" Though some Men should not find it relish'd high enough for their finer Wits, or warmer Pallats, it will not perhaps be useless to those of lower Flights.'

WILLIAM PENN, 1702.

# 1 LEAVE THAT BOOK

His thoughts said, I have been reading a spiritual book and I am confused and tired with trying to understand.

His Father said, Leave that book and read the Book that thou lovest best ; thou wilt find it much simpler.

# 2 FLIES

His thoughts said, When I would seek Him whom my soul loveth, confusions like flies buzz about me.

His Father said, Press through these confusions as thou wouldest press through a swarm of gnats. Take no notice of them. Be not stayed by them. Be not occupied with them. Be not entangled by them.

# 3 THE QUARRY

His thoughts said, The time of preparation for service is longer than I had imagined it would be, and this kind of preparation is difficult to understand.

His Father said, Think of the quarry whence came the stone for My house in Jerusalem.

## 4 THE TOOLS

His thoughts said, I wonder why these special tools are used?

His Father said, The house, when it was in building, was built of stone made ready before it was brought thither ; so that there was neither hammer nor axe nor any tool of iron heard in the house, while it was in building.

If thou knewest the disappointment it is to the builders when the stone cannot be used for the house, because it was not made ready before it was brought thither, if thou knewest My purpose for thee, thou wouldest welcome any tool if only it prepared thee quietly and perfectly to fit into thy place in the house.

The son knew that if he came to serve the Lord he must prepare his soul for temptation ; but he had never expected the particular temptation that confronted him now.

His Father asked him if he had expected to choose his temptations. The son said, No ; but he longed to have done with temptation for ever. His Father said, One day it shall be so. As a dream when one awaketh, so it will be. That dream will never come again. But thou must learn to endure and to conquer. Blessed is the man that endureth temptation. And He told him of the hidden manna prepared for the overcomer. Watch for the hidden manna, He said, it will come in hidden ways. Then to the son it was given to taste of the manna hidden in a word he had not found before : " Put your trust in the Lord God, and ye shall be trusted." The son was greatly delighted with that word, and he prayed that he might be made worthy of so great a thing as the trust of his Father.

## 6 PRESS ON, PRESS ON TO THE SUMMIT

His thoughts said, The coil of circumstances is beyond anything I ever experienced before.

His Father said, All this assemblage of complicated circumstances is the massif of the mountains thou must climb. There is a way among the boulders of the moraine, between the seracs of the glaciers, over the snow-bridges that cross the crevasses, round the overhanging snow-fields and up the precipices and long aretes. There is a way through the deep shadows that will seem to bar thy path at times. Press on, press on to the summit.

## 7 IS THINE HEART SET ON ASCENTS?

His thoughts said, The rocks are far too steep for me. I cannot climb.

His Father said, With Me as thy Guide, thou canst. I have not given thee the spirit of fear, but of power and of love and of discipline. Whence then this spirit of fear?

His thoughts said, But who shall ascend into the hill of the Lord or who shall rise up in His holy Place? Shall I ever pass the foothills?

His Father said, Is thine heart set on ascents?

The son answered, O Lord, Thou knowest.

And the Father comforted him, Commit thy way—thy way to the summit—to thy Lord. Only let thine heart be set on ascents.

And the Father added, Dear son, I will keep thine heart set on ascents.

## 8 THE SECRET PLACE OF THE STORM

After a time of tension his thoughts said, It is written of David, David was dispirited. I am dispirited. I cannot speak to any one of the cause. It is private.

His Father said, I heard thee in the secret place of the storm. In the secret place among the unspoken things, there am I.

The son answered, When I am poor and

in heaviness, Thy help, O Lord, doth lift
me up.

And his Father said, Cast not away
therefore thy confidence which hath great
recompense of reward.


## 9 BITTER WATER

His thoughts said, As I journey, sometimes the water is bitter.

His Father said, Let My loving Spirit
lead thee forth into the land of righteousness. Do not ask Him whether He will
lead thee to Marah or to Elim. Do not
ask for the Elims of life. If thou must
pass through Marah, fear not, for He will
show thee a Tree, which, when thou shalt
cast it into the waters, shall make the
bitter waters sweet. One thought of
Calvary will make any water sweet.


## 10 DURING SLEEP

The son wished to continue his journey
while he was asleep, and to be as near to
his Lord during sleep as when he was

awake ; and he wished to awaken into the love of his Lord.

His Father showed him a mother who all through a long journey had carried her little child in her arms, whether it were asleep or awake, so that it travelled on in sleep. And He said, I have made and I will bear, even I will carry.

His Father told him also that if he fell asleep peacefully resting upon some word of peace, he would awaken into love.

## I MIST

His thoughts said, I would not seek for deliciousness and yet I fear lest a mist come between me and the Face whose light is my life.

His Father said, If the mist be the deadly mist of sin, hasten thee to the Cleanser; confess and be forgiven. Then as the mist of the morning flieth before the light of day so shall that mist disappear. But if it be a mist of weariness, be patient. Ye have need of patience. Let patience have her perfect work. Do not mar that work by impatience. Be patient through the dim days. They will pass.

## 12 SUNBEAM AND RAINBOW

The son remembered how straightly a ray of sunlight will cleave through dusty air, and he knew that the dust could never forbid the sunbeam ; it could only serve to make visible the straight path of that ray. And he thought of the words, The bow shall be seen in the cloud, and he knew that always in past times when mistiness had perplexed action, sooner or later a rainbow had appeared.

Pondering this he found strong consolation.

## 13 DARKNESS

His thoughts said, A sudden darkness descendeth.

His Father said, On which side of the Cloud of My Providence art thou living? The cloud that was darkness to the Egyptians gave light by night to My people. Is it night with thee ? Doth the

shadow of fear that thou wilt give way
begin to creep over thy spirit? Look up.
The Cloud of My Presence is made known
by the Cloud of My Providence, and for
thee in any darkness that cloud will be
light.

## 14 A POWER THAT WAS NOT OF EARTH

His thoughts said, My heart is overwhelmed.

His Father said, Thou art not the first
to feel so. Here is a word for thee,
" When my spirit was overwhelmed within
me, then Thou knewest my path."

And his Father poured comfort into him
saying, O man greatly beloved, Fear not:
peace be unto thee, be strong ; yea, be
strong. And when He had spoken unto
him, the son was strengthened.

Then he remembered how often at midnight, or in the small hours of the morning
when all life's mole-hills become mountains,
some familiar Scripture flowing through
the mind had renewed his strength. And

he knew that in those words was a power that was not of earth.

## 15 WHEN THOU PASSEST. WHEN THOU WALKEST

As the son went on he had to cross rough waters, but before he stepped into the swirl his Father said to him, When thou passest through the waters, I will be with thee ; and through the rivers, they shall not overflow thee. Later, when fiery trials came, When thou walkest through the fire, thou shalt not be burned; neither shall the flame kindle upon thee, was the word on which he lived.

And in grateful wonder the son said, O Father of spirits, Thou dost wonderfully shine forth from the everlasting mountains. The inward thought of man shall give thanks to Thee ; and the memorial of his inward thought shall keep a feast to Thee.

## 16 KNOWING ONLY TO FOLLOW

His thoughts said, How can I know that it is the time to move ?

His Father said, And it shall be when thou shalt hear a sound of going in the tops of the mulberry trees, that then thou shalt go out to battle. Thou shalt certainly hear that sound. There will be a quiet sense of sureness and a sense of peace.

The son said, If another also heard that sound it would be easier.

His Father said, That may not always be. The sound of going is like the voice of the shepherd that the sheep know, but how they know they could not tell, knowing only to follow.

## THE TOKEN

The son said, But how be sure ?

His Father said, When He putteth forth His own sheep, He goeth before them, and the sheep follow Him ; for they know His Voice. And a stranger will they not follow, but will flee from him ; for they know not the voice of strangers. Therein lies the token. Thou wilt recognise the Voice of the Shepherd. The voice of the stranger will be nothing to thee.

His thoughts said, I wish that the sea might be made into dry land and the waters divide—then all would understand that Thou art leading me.

His Father said, That crossing of the sea was the first and the easier obedience. The crossing of the river later on asked for a more daring faith. The way did not open in Jordan till the feet of the priests were dipped in the water. But it did open then. Rivers turn to roads, mountains become valleys, when He who is named the Remover of Hindrances goeth before. Then no one can forbid. No power can bar the way.

## 19 NOT OF DOUBLE HEART

But the son still wondered what he should do if he did not hear a Voice directing him, till he came to understand that, as he waited, his Father would work and would so shape the events of common life that they would become indications of His will. He was shown also that they would be in

accord with some word of Scripture which
would be laid upon his heart.  This Scripture in the light of these events, and these
events in the light of that Scripture, would
work together under the hand of his
Father, and point in the same direction.
And as he followed step by step the way
would open before him.  Only he was
warned to be careful that his eye be single.
He must be like David's soldiers, who were
not of double heart.


## LOVE AND THOU SEEST

The son thought of Absalom, who dwelt
two full years in Jerusalem and saw not the
King's face.  What if he be like Absalom ?

And he remembered Bartimaeus, and
how, casting away his garment, he sprang
up and came to the Lord Jesus.  Was
there a garment that he had not cast away ?

His Father said, O foolish one and blind,
if there be any hindering thing known to
thee, cast it away now ;  if such there be
and thou dost not know it, I will discover
it to thee.  Be not anxious even about

that. Dost thou not love? I know that
thou lovest. Love and thou comest. Love
and thou seest.

## 21 TOO WONDERFUL FOR ME

His thoughts said, There are days when
little things go wrong, one after another,
and, like poor Martha, I am distracted
by much serving. Such days are very
trying.

His Father said, On such days take to
thyself the words of thy Saviour which
thou hast so often given to others. Let
them be thy solace and thy tranquillity.
But tell Me, when thou art under pressure,
dost thou turn first to thy companions or
to Me? Thy companions hearken to thy
voice: cause *Me* to hear it. Let *Me* see
thy countenance, let *Me* hear thy voice.

And the son said, Such love as Thine is
too wonderful for me: it is high, I cannot
attain unto it, but I stretch forth my
hands unto Thee.

His thoughts said, The way is rough.

His Father said, But every step bringeth thee nearer to thy Home.

His thoughts said, The fight is fierce.

His Father said, He who is near to his Captain is sure to be a target for the archers.

His thoughts said, The night is long.

His Father said, But joy cometh in the morning.

## 3 AS IN A DAY OF FEASTING

The son prayed, Let them that love Thee be as the sun when he goeth forth in his might. Let all tediousness of spirit pass from me. But he felt tedious in spirit.

Then upon his listening ear quiet words distilled as the dew : '' He shall bring joy upon thee, and shall refresh thee with His love ; and He shall rejoice over thee with delight as in a day of feasting.''

15

The son remembered how when he was a very little child he had sympathized with the grey sea. The blue sea was a happy sea. The green sea, when the waves thereof tossed themselves and roared, was a triumphant sea. But the grey sea looked anxious. So the child was sorry for the grey sea. Grey weather he abhorred.

Something of this feeling was with him still. Grey weather was not among the things for which he gave thanks.

His Father said to him, All weathers nourish souls.

## 25 TRAVELLER'S JOY

The son asked that he and his fellow-travellers might find the plant called Traveller's Joy. But did it grow alongside every road?

His Father told him that it did; for by every road where His travellers walked He had sown some seeds of light, and those seeds springing up became Traveller's Joy.

His Father also showed him that everything he touched was meant to be a source of joy : Ye shall rejoice in all the things on which ye shall lay your hand.

## AS A CORIANDER SEED

His thoughts said, I feel famished.

His Father said, This need never be. The Lord will not suffer the soul of His servant to famish. Art thou early enough upon the ground when I rain bread from heaven ? In the morning the dew lay round about the host, and when the dew that lay was gone up, behold, upon the face of the wilderness there lay a small round thing, as small as hoar-frost on the ground. Are thine eyes open to see just a little thing, as little as a coriander seed ?

## WHEN THE DEW FELL IN THE NIGHT

The son said, Thinking of manna I feel reproached. So many hours are spent merely in sleep.

17

His Father said, When the dew fell in the night, the manna fell upon it. While thou sleepest I prepare heavenly food for thee. But it is written, " The people shall go out and gather a day's portion every day ; " and one who watched the birds and beasts and fishes said, "That Thou givest them, they gather." Thou hast thy part to do. Go out, then, and gather thy portion for to-day. Thou canst not live upon yesterday's portion.

## 28 HEM IT WITH QUIETNESS

His thoughts said, What if I have not much time to gather my portion ?

His Father said, Hast thou only one minute ? Hem it with quietness. Do not spend it in thinking how little time thou hast. I can give thee much in one minute.

Then the son remembered the Jewish tradition about the manna and the dew. The manna fell on the dew, they said, then more dew fell on the manna so that it was found between two layers of dew. And he thought of the quietness of dew and of how

far it was removed from bustle of any kind.
And he understood the word that his
Father had spoken to him.

## 9 LITTLE SIPS

The son wondered how it would be if
because of press of business or illness he
could not go out early in the morning to
gather his portion.

His Father understood, and he caused
him to know that if the business concerned
the Kingdom, or if illness or any such real
hindrance interrupted, he should be at
rest. Only he was warned to be careful
lest the interruption should slide into a
custom. He was not meant to be easy
with himself.

But he was reminded that the living
water was never out of reach. If he had
not time to drink long in the morning, he
could take little sips now and then through
the day from the Brook that is always
flowing in the way.

## 30 A SONG OF LOVELY THINGS

The son greatly wished to make a Song of Lovely Things to sing to his Beloved, but he could not find singing-words. Then he heard a Voice saying, Thou art walking in the road where all My lovers walked, and some of them walked singing. They have left their songs behind them. Find them. Sing them. They will be thine to Me.

But the lover was grieved because he found no words, neither his own nor those of others ; and yet his mind did truly desire to ascend. While feeling so, he read, On Thee praise waiteth all hushed, O God, in Zion ; and He who is Love Eternal said, I will be silent in My love. And he entered into Silence and met Love Eternal there.

After a while there was a sound of gentle stillness and it said, Thy silence is to Me a Song of Lovely Things.

## 31 I WILL REMEMBER

His thoughts said, The Lord is my strength and my shield; my heart trusted in Him, and I am helped, and yet at times the waves sweep up and almost overwhelm me and I feel like Job, Thou dissolvest my substance.

His Father said, At such times say to thyself, " I will remember the years of the Right hand of the Most High, I will remember the days of old." Have the waves ever covered thee ? Hast thou ever sunk as lead in the mighty waters ? As it was, so it is ; as it hath been, so it shall be. And in the end, with Mine own hands, I will bring thee unto thy desired haven.

## 2 NO CONDEMNATION

His thoughts said, There is no foundation for hope in anything but Calvary.

His Father said, That is true. But Calvary is an eternal fact. Thou hast been redeemed with the precious Blood, as of a Lamb without blemish and without spot, even the Blood of Christ. Didst thou pray, " Wash me throughly " ? Then I did wash thee throughly. I have cast all thy sins into the depths of the sea. Who ever found anything again which was cast into those depths? I have pleaded the cause of thy soul. There is no condemnation to them which are in Christ Jesus. Now, forgetting the things that are behind, press on.

## 33 JACOB, JACOB

His thoughts said, There are some things that I cannot forget.

His Father said, The humbling memory will help thee to walk softly with Me and tenderly with others. But even so there is relief from all distress. O thou that art named the house of Jacob, is the Spirit of the Lord straitened? When I spoke unto Israel in the visions of the night, I did not use that glorious name; I used the old name which had so sorrowful a meaning. I said, "Jacob, Jacob," and he answered, "Here am I."

Jacob, Jacob, the deceiver, the supplanter, that name is a reminder of thy fall, but also and far more of My mercy. It is to thee I am speaking, to thee, not to another,

worthier one, but to thee, My child—
*Jacob, Jacob.*

## LET MY LOVE RESTORE

His thoughts said, I am not what I
meant to be, or what others think I am.

His Father said, It is written, "He
restoreth my soul. The Law of the Lord
is perfect, restoring the soul." Let some
word of Mine restore thee. Let My love
restore thee. Didst thou think thou hadst
a Father who did not know that His child
would need to be restored ? I will restore
health unto thee : I will heal thee of thy
wounds. I will restore comforts unto thee.
I will restore unto thee the joy of My
salvation. I will renew a right spirit
within thee. I will not cast thee away
from My Presence.

Child of My love, trust thy Father. If
the Spirit speaketh some word in thy heart,
obey that word. And, or ever thou art
aware, thou wilt know thyself restored.

## 35 LOST YEARS

His thoughts said, But the lost years, what of them ?

His Father said, I will restore to thee the years that the locust hath eaten, the cankerworm and the caterpillar and the palmer worm. I know the names of all the insects and worms which have devoured thy beauty and thy power. I will deal with them all, and cause thee to help others in danger of like injury. So shall thy years be restored.

## 36 BE STILL AND THOU SHALT HEAR

The son's troubled thoughts could not see how one so marred could ever be of use, but he remembered the comforting figure of the potter who did not throw away the clay that was marred in his hands, but made it again another vessel.

And his Father said, Take some promise of Mine, fulfil the condition attached thereto, and thou shalt be astonished at the change that will be wrought in thee.

The son asked why he did not hear more clearly and more constantly the pleasant Voice of the Mighty One ; to which his Father answered, There was a Voice from the firmament that was over their heads, when they stood, and had let down their wings. The wings of thy work, the wings of thy will, the wings of thine inmost longing, the wings of thy cherished desire— let them down. Be still, and thou shalt hear.

## 7 IN THE LIGHT OF THY COUNTENANCE IS LIFE

The son found himself in a barren place.

His Father said, In this place will I give peace, and there I will nourish thee. Son, thou art ever with Me, and all that I have is thine. And his Father with great gentleness drew him to Himself, saying, I humbled thee, and suffered thee to hunger, and fed thee with manna ; that I might make thee know that man doth not live by bread only; but by every word that proceedeth out of the mouth of the Lord doth

man live.   Then the son said, Lord, evermore give me this Bread.

When he thirsted his Father said, The
Lord will not suffer the soul of His servant
to famish. And the son answered, O
Thou who art the Gladness of my exultation, in the light of Thy countenance is
life.

## 38 EXPERIENCE WORKETH POWER TO HELP

The son greatly wondered why one so
generously succoured could ever feel poor
and needy and thirsty.

His Father asked him four questions :

Can he who hath never thirsted know
the preciousness of water?

Can he who hath not found rivers on
bare heights lead his fellow to those rivers?

Can he who hath not walked in the deep
valleys of the spirit help the fainting to
find fountains?

Can he who hath never seen the glowing
sand become a pool bear witness to the
marvel of My power?

# THERE IS NO OTHER WAY

His thoughts said, Is there no other way of learning how to help another but by the way of suffering?

His Father said, Had there been another way, would I not have found it for the Son of My love, whom no thorn of pain had ever pierced, who was tender as a child to the touch ? If it became Me in bringing many sons unto glory, to lead the Captain of their salvation by that way, wouldest thou win souls without a pang ? Settle it once for all ; there is no other way.

# NOT EVEN A CUP OF TEA

The son said, My heart is disquieted within me. My soul cleaveth to the dust. Out of the depths have I cried unto Thee, O God.

His Father said, In My hand are the deep places of the earth. Is there no blue sky ? Have roses forgotten how to blow ? Have birds ceased to sing among the branches ? Hast thou not the sweetness of the love of a single little child ? Hast thou no pleasant food—not even a cup of tea ? Have tears been thy meat day and night ?

Gather up thy comforts, the greatest, the smallest, and thou wilt be surprised that thou hast so many to gather.


41 WHILE WE LOOK NOT AT . . .
    BUT AT . . .

His thoughts said, The affairs of the present press so closely upon me, that I cannot live as one should who is seeking a better Country, that is, an heavenly. I am bound to earth by very many ties. The things I hear fill my ears, the things I see fill my eyes.

His Father said, Read again the words thou hast often read before about the things that are seen and the things that are not seen. Ponder the word *while*. Let the power of this revelation penetrate thy soul.

# THE HEALING OF THE TONGUE

His thoughts said, Nothing that I have been able to say to those whom I have tried to help seemed to do much for them. What is the use of saying anything ? Perhaps it would be better to say nothing.

His Father said, The healing of the tongue is a tree of Life. Hast thou ever seen a tree bear fruit in a day?


# IS IT MY CUSTOM TO FORGET ?

In the late evening the son looked back over the day and was discouraged. But as one whom his mother comforteth, so did his Father comfort him. He said to him, Didst thou not in the early morning bear upon thy heart thy beloved ones, as Aaron bore the jewels on his breast? Didst thou not offer to Me every hour of the day, every touch on other lives, every letter to be written, everything to be done ? As the hours passed over thee perhaps thou didst forget ; but is it *My* custom to forget?

His thoughts said, If it were any one else I should not feel so doubtful.

His Father said, Because thou art what thou knowest thou art and what I know thou art, the glory will be all Mine when anything is done.  Look not at thyself at all ; let thine eyes be ever looking unto thy Lord.

Then in grateful wonder the son said, Thy lovingkindness is ever before mine eyes.

And his Father said, Conceal not My lovingkindness.


## 45 WHO IS THIS THAT COMETH UP FROM THE WILDERNESS ?

The son knew that his Father's desire was to deck His priests with health and joy and vigour.  A wilderness experience did not seem to be His choice for them, and yet for many the wilderness was appointed. The son was perplexed about this.  Then the Spirit, the Comforter, brought to his mind words from the Gospels about his

Lord's sojourn in the wilderness, and the figure of the true in the Song of Songs : *Who is this that cometh out of the Wilderness?* And he saw that no child of the Father was asked to walk where the footsteps of his Lord were not clear on the road. But he saw also that always there was a coming out of the wilderness: *Who is this that cometh up from the wilderness leaning upon her Beloved?* No dwelling-place was ever built in any wilderness for any child of God.

## 5 NOT A NEW WORD TO THEE

The son said, The children of Ephraim being armed and carrying bows turned back in the day of battle. I am armed. I have no excuse for a single backward look. O make my spirit stedfast with Thee.

His Father said, Thy help standeth in the Name of the Lord who hath made heaven and earth.

The son answered earnestly, Stablish the thing, O God, that Thou hast wrought in me. And yet his thoughts persisted, But

31

if I slip ? The God of all patience answered,
Then Love, travelling in the greatness of
His strength, will gather thee up. There
is nothing that Love will not do for thee.
"When I said, my foot slippeth, Thy
mercy, O Lord, held me up," is not a new
word to thee.

## 47 WOULD IT MATTER ?

His thoughts said, My work is not im-
portant. Would it matter very much if a
floor were left unswept or a room left un-
tidied ? Or if I forgot to put flowers for a
guest, or omitted some tiny unimportant
courtesy ?

His Father said, Would it have mattered
very much if a few people had been left
without wine at a feast ? But thy Lord
turned water into wine for them.

And the son remembered the words,
*Jesus took a towel*.

## 48 SOME CROPS MUST BE HANDPICKED

His thoughts said, When I hear of wonderful things done elsewhere I am glad, and

yet with the gladness is unsettlement of
mind. There is a strange allure in all I
hear. There are days when I fly from the
place where I am to the place where souls
are flocking to Thee. There is a wavering
in me which I do not understand.

His Father said, This wavering is a
temptation. Many have known it. Thy
times are in My hand. Thy time to-day is
in My hand. Would I waste My servant's
time ? Remember thy Lord's hour by the
well. He who sent thee is with thee.
Not all fields are reaped with the sickle.
Some crops must be hand-picked.

9 DWELL DEEP

His thoughts said, My longing is to heal
the broken and the weak, to defend the
maimed, and to lead the blind unto the
sight of the glory of the Lord. My choice
is to be a corn of wheat and fall into the
ground and die. Then why these waver-
ings ?

His Father said, Too much of thy surface
is exposed to the breath of every wind that

33

bloweth. Thou must learn to dwell deep.

And the son who had wavered answered humbly, Renew within me a settled spirit. Establish me with Thy directing Spirit. My heart is fixed, O God, my heart is fixed. I will sing and give praise.

## 50 I AM THE GOD OF THINE EXPECTATION AND THY HOPE

His thoughts said, It is too much to hope that such a one as I should truly please my Lord.

His Father said, But it is written, " It is God which worketh in you both to will and to do of His good pleasure." In My servant Paul I wrought an earnest expectation and a hope, that in nothing he should be ashamed, but that always Christ should be magnified in his body. I am the God of thine expectation and thy hope.

## 51 THOU ART MY SHELL

The son said, But, my Father, Thou knowest that I am not St. Paul.

His Father said, Hast thou watched a wave fill a shell on the shore ? Thou art My shell. Wave upon wave I will flow over thee, poor empty shell that thou art. So shalt thou be filled with the fullness of the sea. For I am able to give thee an overflowing measure of all good gifts, that all thy wants of every kind may be supplied at all times, and thou mayest give of thine abundance to every good work.

## 2 ASHAMED ON MY ACCOUNT

The son said to his Father, If this new campaign to which I am committed come to grief, then some who trusted me, believing that Thou wert leading me, will be ashamed. Let not them that wait on Thee, O Lord of hosts, be ashamed on my account.

The Father said to His son, They shall not be ashamed that wait on Me. And the son said to himself, Return unto thy rest, O my soul, for the Lord hath dealt bountifully with thee. I will sing of the Lord because He hath dealt so lovingly with me.

## 53 IF ANY LACK, LET HIM ASK

His thoughts said, Suddenly a question is asked, suddenly a decision must be made. The answer and the decision affect the lives of others. In me is no wisdom at all. Sometimes it is as if I could not even pray.

His Father said, A breath may be a prayer; I hide not Mine ear at thy breathing. But be a simple child with Me. Ask for the thing that thou needest most. I will not upbraid thee. If any lack wisdom, let him ask. And as thou goest on thy way thou shalt do as occasion serve thee; for God is with thee. Dost thou lack strength ? The Lord of hosts shall be for strength to them that turn the battle at the gate.

## 54 FENNEL AND CUMMIN

The son felt that if the matter were one of warfare he would not be anxious. There are great promises for warriors. The matter just then on his mind was smaller than that, and yet a mistake might injure a soul. And he mourned over past failures.

Then he remembered, fennel and cummin, wheat and barley and spelt, each a small grain, but not forgotten in his Father's counsel to farmers. He found comfort also in the assurance, *He that is perfect in knowledge is with thee.* And he believed that he would be taught how to train aright each of those committed to his care, for his God would teach him; for this also cometh forth from the Lord of hosts, which is wonderful in counsel and excellent in working. Thus, casting his burden upon the Lord, he was nourished, and received from the God of Hope all joy and peace in believing ; that he might abound in hope through the power of the Holy Ghost.

## 5 STAND STILL IN JORDAN

The son felt that his days were becoming a breathless rush.

His Father searched him with questions : What of the minutes before the rush of the day is upon thee ? Art thou filling them too full ? Thy day may indeed be as

Jordan that overfloweth all his banks
all the time of harvest ; but when thou
comest to the brink of the water of Jordan
dost thou stand still in Jordan ?  Rise
from thy knees and stand.  Stand still and
know that I am God.  Stand still and
know that I am Peace.  Give Me time to
bathe thee in peace.  Then, as the brim-
ming hours pass by thee, give Me time to
renew thee in peace.


## 56 PEACE ALWAYS IN ALL CONDITIONS

His thoughts said, If only things continued in a regular order I should find it
much easier to maintain a restful spirit, but
as it is, there is no continuance in anything,
ever.

His Father said, Think it not strange if it
be so.  Thou hast here no continuing city,
thou art seeking one to come.  These
changes are merely the changeful landscape
of thy life as thou travellest to the City
which hath foundations.  But thy journey
may be restful ; if thou art inwardly at
rest nothing outward can disturb thee.

Peace always under all conditions—that is my word for thee. Do not let it slip. Do not drift away from it. Hold it fast; for it is not a vain thing for thee; because it is thy life.

# 7 INTERRUPTIONS

The son wondered how it could be possible to sit in heavenly places in Christ Jesus when life was so full of interruptions. Hardly an hour was without something that broke its ordered flow.

One day as he sat by a mountain stream he noticed the lovely way of water when interrupted by the boulders that broke its ordered flow. The river turned each into an occasion for beauty. And he understood that it was possible to live the river's way if only he took the interrupting things, not as interruptions, but as opportunities, and indeed as very part of life.

And while he sat there by the water, his dear Lord said to him, As the ripples of the river glance up to the light, let thy heart glance up to Me in little looks of love very often through the day.

## 58 EVEN MINE

The son said, Every day my enemy seeketh my soul to destroy it ; O God, my Saviour, overlook me not.

His Father said, Saul sought David every day, but I did not deliver him into his hands. I will not overlook thee. Am I not mightier than ten thousand Sauls ?

And the son remembered the words, They that be with us are more than they that be with them. There is a greater with us than with him. Greater is He that is in you than he that is in the world. And he said, The Lord is my Rock and my Fortress and my Deliverer, even mine.

## 59 THY REREWARD

There was a time when the thoughts of the son saw the foe as a pursuing host.

His Father said, Am I not thy Rereward ? The Angel of the Lord which went before the camp of Israel removed and went behind them. It shall be again as it was long ago when I blew My wind and the sea covered the pursuing host. Fear not therefore. Thou shalt know whether My word will overtake thee or not.

And the son knew that long before the foe could overtake him, the Power of his God would overtake and enfold him. And he said, My soul trusteth in Thee ; and, under the shadow of Thy wings shall be my refuge until this tyranny be over-past.

## WITH YOU EFFECTUALLY

But again his thoughts said, Terrific powers are set in array against me.

His Father said, And thou art as a little child who knoweth not how to meet them. But with thee is a Stronger than they. Do not forget to sing : When they began to sing and to praise, the Lord set ambushments. Because the hand of Amalek is against the throne of the Lord, the Lord will have war with Amalek from generation to generation. Therefore be not afraid nor be discouraged by reason of this great multitude. The Lord thy God, He shall fight against them together with you effectually.

His thoughts said, But what of to-morrow ?

His Father said, Thus saith the Lord to thee, even thee, Fear not. Fear not, neither be afraid to go forth to-morrow. No evil shall be sent to meet thee. But the son knew that trouble might be sent to meet him.

His Father said, Before the trouble can meet thee it must pass through the brightness of My encompassing Presence, and passing through that brightness it loseth its darkness. It hath no more any power for evil. Also, as thou knowest well, I will be with thee in trouble.

On this word the son stayed his heart, saying, *The Lord will take care of me.* I will trust and not be afraid to go forth to-morrow. I will praise Thee, O Lord, for it is a good thing to sing praises to Thee, yea, a joyful and pleasant thing it is to be thankful. And he marvelled that he had ever been afraid.

## 2 I DREAMT

His thoughts said, I dreamt a distressing dream last night. I was threatened with torture for Christ's sake, but I escaped it. I did not endure.

His Father said, When did I promise to give strength and grace in a dream of the night ? My grace is for that which *is*, not for that which may never be.

## 3 GRACE TO HELP IN TIME OF NEED

Then the son was caused to understand that just as his dream had deluded him, so, very often his imagination had misled him. He remembered the assurance, Thou wilt keep him in perfect peace whose imagination is stayed on Thee because he trusteth in Thee ; and he knew that he must learn to discipline his mind and its powers of imagination. If this happen, or that, what then ? But if neither happen ? The imagined need is not a need at all.

And the son fastened his faith upon words which were indeed as silver tried in a furnace of earth, purified seven times: *Let us therefore come boldly, that we may find grace to help in time of need.*

## 64  I WILL PERFECT THINE IMPERFECTIONS

His thoughts said, I am ashamed because of my poverty of love and my interrupted obedience.

His Father said, I know it all.  I know thee as thou art and yet I love thee.

His thoughts said, I often pray to be delivered from slothfulness that all the spaces of my time may be fruitfully filled by Thee; and yet the spaces seem to me quite empty, and the little that is done is so imperfectly done that I am ashamed.

His Father said, Commit thine empty spaces to Me, and let thy trust be in the tender mercy of thy God for ever and ever. I will perfect thine imperfections.

## 65  MUCH INCENSE

Very often the thoughts of the son spoke thus : How can I offer my poor work to my holy Lord? Holy, holy, holy, is the Lord of hosts. I see His holiness as fire, white as purity. I see my work as dust. Who can understand his errors? Cleanse Thou me from secret faults. Keep back Thy servant also from presumptuous sins. Let them not have dominion over me. Is not even the thought of offering dust of earth to the Lord of heaven a presumptuous sin? And the son was about to withdraw the work which he had brought.

But he saw the Cross, and a Voice spoke: Lay thy dust in the dust at the foot of the Cross. And he did so.

Then he saw the likeness of an angel who stood by a golden altar having a golden censer, and there was given unto him much incense that he should offer it with the prayers of all saints upon the golden altar.

And he was caused to understand that the Much Incense of the merits of his Saviour sufficed for work as well as for prayer. And he offered his handful of dust.

The son went a day's journey into the wilderness, and there he found a juniper tree, where he sat down, and he said, Let it be enough. And behold, Some One touched him. And in that Touch was Life.

Then the son said to his Father, Blessed be God who hath never turned away my prayer nor His mercy from me. O let me show how true the Lord my strength is. And his Father, giving patience to the faint-hearted and life to the broken-hearted, healed him and comforted him. And the son rose up in vigour and served his Lord again.

## 67 THEY FOUGHT WITH GLADNESS

The son, considering the life-stories of explorers, scientists and others in whom is the great quality of valour, and also the many patient toilers of the earth, noticed that all were one in accepting the conditions of their calling as a matter of course.

Why then did the follower of a Leader

who never offered ease, so often make much of trials he met in the way?

And remembering certain ancient words, *They fought with gladness the battles of Israel*, the son desired to be one of that great company.

## 8  LIKE A FLINT

The son said, I am nothing.  His Father said, Did I ever tell thee that thou wert something ?

The son said, But I do not feel fit for this that is given to me to do.  His Father said, Canst thou not trust Me to make thee fit ?

The son said, But I am not successful. His Father said, At the end of the day will My word be, Come, thou good and successful servant ?  If only thou wilt walk humbly with thy God it will be, Come, thou good and *faithful* servant.

The son said, But I do not care for what I have to do.  His Father answered, At last thou hast touched the root of the matter. Did thy Saviour '' care for '' Calvary ?

Then the Eternal Spirit opened to him those terrible Scriptures which show Gethsemane and Calvary, till all his paltry " Buts " were shrivelled as withered leaves in the fire. And he saw Him whom he followed as He set His face like a flint ; and he was utterly confounded and ashamed.

## 69 FROTH

His thoughts said, It is strange how often the scourge of the tongue is the cause of difficult travelling. And he said, Words, words, words—how futile they are, but how bewildering they can be, and how grieving, how breaking ! How long will ye vex my soul and break me in pieces with words ?

His Father said, The noise of words, the dust of words, the wind of words, they are not worth thy grief. Wilt thou grieve over them to-morrow ? Thou wilt have forgotten them. Forget them now. They are froth.

But as he went on doing his appointed work the son found that sometimes it was impossible to avoid the froth of words. He was taught then to seek in that froth for anything of value. There might be something even in ignorant words which would help him to do his work better. As for the rest, he learned that, like the molten images of heathendom, there was no breath in them, they were vanity, the work of delusion, they would perish. His wisdom lay in going on quietly, not turning aside for any man's talk, loving the talkers if they cared for his love, refusing to take up a reproach against any. Life is too short for animosities.

## NOTICE THE SILENCE OF THY LORD

His thoughts said, It is difficult to bear with injustice and rudeness, especially when directed towards a courteous and noble-hearted friend.

His Father said, If the rudeness be toward a friend, commit him to Me. I

will be his shield and his exceeding great
Reward. If it be toward thee, remember
thy Lord. He never met rudeness with
rudeness : He ignored it. But He ob-
served it, and being very man, He suffered
under it. He felt as thou feelest—yet
without sin. Notice His silence : He was
often silent. Notice His speech : it was
never struck from Him by a rude act. His
words were spoken in gentleness of spirit,
after a pause : Thou gavest Me no water
for My feet. Thou gavest Me no kiss.

## 72 COME UNTO ME AND I WILL
REFRESH THEE

His thoughts said, I can no longer.

His Father said, Thou canst. Thou
canst do all things through Christ which
strengtheneth thee. Is tribulation a new
thing to any child of Mine ? Shouldest
thou expect to be without pressure, batter-
ings, toil, tears, discouragements, dis-
appointments, ingratitudes, obloquies ? All
My servants had these in abundant measure.
Look and thou wilt see their footsteps in the

dust of the road. But they had strong consolation and so hast thou. Not to be pitied, but happy is he that hath the God of Jacob for his help, whose hope is in the Lord his God.

Doth the burning sun distress thee ? There shall be a shadow from the heat. Art thou beaten by the storm ? There shall be a covert for thee from storm and from rain. Or is it that thou art too weary to know why thou art so weary ? Then come unto Me and I will refresh thee.

## 3 THE STUNG AND THE STINGER

His thoughts said, The sting of the grief abideth.

His Father said, My word to thee is, " Pray for them which despitefully use thee." The word is not, " Wait till the stinger be sorry for stinging." Art thou stung ? Thou wilt find as thou prayest that the sting will lose its power. Thy thinking will be kindly. Thou wilt remember Him who, when He was reviled, reviled not again ; when He suffered, He

threatened not ; but committed Himself
to Him that judgeth righteously Thy
Saviour hath left thee an example that thou
shouldest follow His steps.

## 74 DO NOT BE UNJUST

The son was troubled, longing that confidence should be restored and yet not seeing
how that which snapped in an hour of stress
could be counted upon again.

His Father opened the matter to him :
Thou canst not recreate confidence. But
do not be unjust. What ground hadst
thou for thy confidence ? Didst thou ask
sand to be rock ? Iron to be steel ? Cane
to be oak ? To do that is to expect what
cannot be. It is to be unjust.

Now turn from these sad thoughts :
think of the faithful and loyal in whom thy
heart may safely rest. Are not their words
as honeycomb, sweet to the soul, and
health to the bones ? Be grateful, make
much of them, and go on thy way as one
who is girded with gladness.

## 5 LEAVE ME TO TAKE CARE OF MY GLORY

His thoughts said, It is the wrong done to others that is most painful. O to comfort them !

His Father said, Lovest thou thy beloved better than He who made them ? I Myself will be their Comforter.

His thoughts said, I am anxious about the good name of my Lord. It cannot be to His glory that untruth should be spread abroad like smoke.

His Father said, Thy part is to walk softly. The smoke of earth cannot reach so high as the place where My honour dwelleth. Leave Me to take care of My glory.

## 6 THOU ART NO BIRD

His thoughts said, Arrows are shot, as it were, from darkness, from nowhere. I cannot see whence they come and I do not know why they are shot. I only know that I long to escape out of their reach.

His Father said, That is not a new temptation.  Meet it as he did who wrote, "How say ye to my soul, Flee as a bird to your mountain ?  They make ready their arrow upon the string that they may shoot in darkness."  Arrows shot in open day can be seen and countered.  Arrows shot in darkness test the temper and poise of the spirit.  But do not flee as a bird.  Thou art no bird.

## 77 SPEECH AND SILENCE

The son was unhappy because he had been compelled to speak of something he greatly wished to wrap in silence.  When should he speak ?  When be silent ?

His Father caused him to understand that when the wrong done was personal, his lips must be silent.  And he must see to it that in the hidden man of the heart there was always the gentleness of Christ.

But when the good of others required it, then he must speak even as Paul did when he wrote of two who turned away, of two whose word ate as doth a canker and of some whose influence hindered. Let Love be without dissimulation.

Then the son took for a law of life these words : "Silence, unless the reason for speech will bear the searchlight of Eternity."

## 8 LET THE REST GO BY

His thoughts said, How wearisome is the chatter of earth.

His Father said, The world passeth away and the lust thereof (and the talk thereof), but he that doeth the will of God abideth for ever. Fix thine heart on the doing of My will and let the rest go by.

## 9 THY GOD BEARETH PATIENTLY WITH THEE

His thoughts said, I looked for clearness in souls. I do not always find it.

His Father said, One day thou shalt look everywhere and see only spirits made perfect, clear as the pure river of water of life, clear as crystal, pure gold as it were transparent glass.

But even now where thou art, as thou well knowest, there are some like that river, that gold. Again I say, rejoice in them. And with others, be patient. Thy God beareth patiently with thee.

## 80 BE OCCUPIED IN THE GREATEST THINGS

The son, though consoled by the love of his Lord, found himself so preoccupied by the grief of disillusionment that he was bound in spirit and not free for his rightful work. But his God uncovered his eyes, and he saw this preoccupation as a bond from which the Spirit of Liberty was waiting to unbind him.

And he knew that he must be occupied in the greatest things. He was doing a great work and he could not come down to these little things. If they did not seem little things to him, he must ask himself this question : Was He, whom he called Master and Lord, always understood ? Was He never misjudged ? They laid to His charge things that He knew not, to the great discomfiture of His spirit. Is it not enough for the disciple to be as his Master and the servant as his Lord ?


## THE GRACE OF CONTINUANCE

The son asked for the Grace of Continuance. His Father showed him a waterfall fed from unseen fountains. The river of God is full of water, was his word then.

The son feared the chilly influences of life. His Father showed him an altar. All night unto the morning the fire burned there. The fire shall ever be burning upon the altar; it shall never go out.

Then the son remembered that as the fall was fed by water from above, so the fire of the altar was lighted by Fire that came from before the Lord.


## 2  THE SECRET OF CONTINUED ENDURANCE

The son asked, What is the secret of continued endurance ?

His Father answered, It is found in seeing

Him who is invisible. It is found in looking at the joy that is set before thee. It is
found in considering Him who endured.
It is found in taking for thine own the words
of one who was tempted to wax faint, " In
the day when I cried Thou answeredst me,
and strengthenedst me with strength in
my soul." It is found in staking thine all
upon the lightest word of the Lord, thy
Redeemer. It is found in loyalty. It is
found in love.


## 83 NOT ONE WOULD BE DISAPPOINTED

The son feared for some who had not any
part or inheritance in the natural joys of
life. He feared loneliness for them.

But his Father said, Fear not to trust
them to Me. I am their Part and their
Inheritance. Would I be a wilderness unto
them, a land of darkness ? Have I ever
been a liar to the heart that trusted Me ?
Have I ever been as waters that fail ?
Thou hast heard their unspoken word,
" My flesh and my heart faileth," and
thy flesh and thy heart faileth too as thou

thinkest of them. Fear not, grieve not.
They will not end on that minor note.
They shall not wear the spirit of heaviness;
they shall wear the garment of praise.  As
the flowers of roses in the spring of the year,
as lilies by the rivers of waters, so shall
their gladness be.  "*But God* is the Strength
of my heart and my Portion for ever"—that
will be their abiding word and their everlasting song.

And the son knew that not one would be
disappointed who had chosen loss for the
sake of the Kingdom of heaven.  And he
was comforted as he thought of those
lovers of his Lord caught up into Paradise,
and hearing words which, could they be
heard now, would not be lawful for a man
to utter.

## 4 TREASURE IN HEAVEN

His thoughts were full of unspoken
longings.

His Father said, Art thou here for
the joy of being together ? Thou hast
Eternity.

The son answered, I know that I have Eternity, but——

His Father said, Is it too hard to sell all that thou hast—even this—that thou mayest have Treasure in heaven?

The son asked to be shown what was meant by Treasure in heaven. He was shown that it meant the greater glory of his Lord, more jewels for His crown, an eternal overweight of joy because of the sword-cut which had set him free to serve without distraction. It meant the holy intimacy foreshadowed by words not yet fully understood, *These are they which follow the Lamb whithersoever He goeth.*

## 85 THY ZEBEDEES WHO ARE MY ZEBEDEES

His thoughts said, I cannot bear that my Zebedees should miss me.

His Father said, They are My Zebedees. One day thou wilt see the first Zebedee who was left with the hired servants. Thou mayest ask him then whether he is sorry that he set his sons free to follow their Saviour. As thy Zebedees are partakers of the suffering, so they are partakers of the consolation. And to all who are called to this fellowship their Lord saith, When I come again I will repay you.

Wouldest thou withhold that from thy Zebedees who are My Zebedees ?

## DO I NOT KNOW THE WAY TO MY OWN COUNTRY ?

The son said, I would not withhold that from them. And well I know that they whom Thou leadest through the deserts do not thirst ; and yet I should be very grateful if there might be no more deserts for them.

His Father said, Do I not know the way to My own Country ? Is it not lawful for Me to do what I will with Mine own ? Once more I say unto thee, Trust My love for thy beloved. No good thing shall I withhold. I will satisfy their soul in drought. I will comfort all their waste places. Am I a God at hand and not a God afar off ?

His thoughts said, I want to pray about all the needs of those whom I love, and how can I, when I am in the dark about them ?

His Father said, But it is not so with Me. No darkness hideth them from Me. Even if thou canst not tell Me what should be done, I know it.

The son feared lest he should forget to pray for some whom he greatly wished to remember.

His Father told him to use common little things as reminders of them. Nothing was too small to be used : "Let the thought of thy friend take wing. It will fly like a homing bird to Me."

The son was glad and grateful about that, but he had a desire to be with his friends, especially in their hours of sorrow and of joy.

His Father said, Think of My two angels. On the day of thy Saviour's Ascension were they among the company that welcomed Him Home ?

I could trust them to do My will elsewhere.

## 8 THERE WILL NOT BE THE TORMENT OF UNCERTAINTY

The son thought of one who seemed to be needed in two places at the same time. Whatever the decision, part of himself must be rent. But most racking of all was the torment of uncertainty.

His Father said, Would an earthly father leave a willing child in doubt about his wishes ? How much less would thy heavenly Father do so unkind a thing ? Must the decision be made to-day ? Then there shall be a sign from Me to-day. Can the matter be deferred ? Then there shall be a going on in quietness. Before action must be taken, I will cause something to happen which will show the way of My choice. Though part of himself be rent, there will be peace which not even that rending can hurt. There will not be the torment of uncertainty.

And the son recalled the peaceful story of the Cloud. Whether it were two days, or a month, or a year, that the Cloud tarried, the people journeyed not : but when it was taken up, they journeyed.

## THE LORD BE BETWEEN ME AND THEE

The thoughts of the son ran thus : Many friendships are weakening. Perhaps it is better to hold aloof from close friendship and to be content with friendliness.

His Father said, The soul of Jonathan was knit to the soul of David, and Jonathan loved him as his own soul. And Jonathan stripped himself even to his sword and to his bow and to his girdle. He went to David into the wood and strengthened his hands in God. "Go in peace," he said on another day, for both of them had sworn saying, "The Lord be between me and thee." And David rose and departed : and Jonathan went into the city.

So the son learned that if only the Lord Himself be the golden bond between heart and heart, all is well. A faithful friend is the medicine of life ; and they that fear the Lord shall find him. And together they shall strive for undefiled rewards.

## SALUTE APELLES

The son thought of many who were living for themselves, travelling here and there for pleasure, spending time and wealth upon personal delights. And he seldom saw them troubled. Life flowed on like a placid stream for them. But others who were pouring out all they possessed in the service of their Lord were perpetually assaulted, and very sorely tried. As he pondered this matter his Father spoke to him saying, Why should one be assaulted who is fighting no battle, and why should one be tried in whom is nothing to be proved ?

Salute Apelles, approved in Christ, (that tested man in Christ). One day thou shalt salute him. Salute him now. The end of that man is peace.

## WINDOWS OF AGATE

The son was grieved because of the dust-storm that had whirled round one of the Lord's Apelles, and the hurricanes that had swept upon another. Long ago he had ceased to ask that any of the Order of Apelles might be kept from trial ; he only asked for strength that they should be fortified. But he was grieved.

His Father showed him that by suffering is wrought stedfastness, and stedfastness is the proof of soundness, and from this proof riseth hope, hope that maketh not ashamed. Accept this by faith, said his Father.

And the son remembered the metal mirrors of old which he had seen in an Eastern land ; nothing was quite clearly reflected. Now we see in a mirror, darkly; we walk by faith, not by sight. We look at life, not through windows of crystal but through windows of agate ; and the purest agate is not perfectly transparent.

## 92 THE COURAGE OF THE LOVE OF THE LORD

The son saw Apelles in the light of a figure of the true : Everything that may abide the fire, ye shall make it go through the fire ; and all that abideth not the fire ye shall make go through the water. He who knew all men and needed not that any should testify of man, because He knew what was in man, knew what could abide the fire, and what could not abide the fire but could abide the water. He Himself knew what He would do with each of His Apelles ; and without Him was not anything done that was done, so that Apelles might be approved in Christ.

And the son wondered not only at the wisdom and the tenderness, but also at the courage of the love of the Lord.

## 3 IS NOT THAT WORTH WHILE ?

The son said, I think of the pain of life that is perpetual for so many who live to serve their fellows. Is it all worth while ?

His Father said, Those who serve their generation are like the sailors that go down to the sea in ships, that do business in great waters. But it is these, not those who play in the shallows, who see the works of the Lord and His wonders in the deep. Is not *that* worth while ?

The son thought of some who received
abundant supplies for their work in answer
to prayer, while others, though equally
prayerful, were often in straits.

The meaning of this matter was opened
to him thus : Those who receive abundantly
have many sharp tests which are secrets
between them and their Lord. The world
knows nothing of them. The appointed
way for them to show forth His glory is
simply to tell out His goodness, and use
His gifts as those who must give account.
But to the others, another and a special
charge is given. No angel ever received
so delicate a charge. For, strengthened
by the Spirit in the inner man, as they
show forth the peace of God amid adverse
circumstances, their fellows watch and
wonder at His grace. The Unseen Beings
of the Heavenly Places watch also, and
adore. To be trusted to live, strengthened
with all might, according to His glorious
power, unto all patience and long suffering
with joyfulness, giving thanks unto the

Father, is the highest trust that can be conferred on man.

## A SON OF KOHATH

The thoughts of the son turned to one upon whose shoulders heavy burdens were constantly laid, while his fellows had much help in the matter of burden-bearing. Then he remembered that in the old days of the Tabernacle Service, Moses took the waggons and the oxen and gave them unto the Levites, but unto the sons of Kohath he gave none ; because the Service of the Sanctuary belonging unto them was that they should bear upon their shoulders. And he knew that even now some were called to be sons of Kohath.

But as he pondered this, there came to his mind a golden word : The beloved of the Lord shall dwell in safety by Him; and the Lord shall cover him all the day long, and he shall dwell between His shoulders. He who is called to bear upon his shoulders the burden of the Service of the Sanctuary, is himself borne. And he knew that it was very good to be a son of Kohath.

The son was troubled because so often, when he wished to lose himself in prayer, his thoughts were not of his Lord but of his children or the turmoil of the world, or the anxieties of his friends, or some problem of the work committed to him, or even of his own concerns.

His Father laid His hand upon him then, and caused him to understand that if only he would turn to Him in worshipping love he would find himself holding his children, life's turmoil, his friends, all problems, in the hush of the Presence of his Lord.   And he would be quiet and free to receive light concerning the matter that lay so close to his heart.   Within a few minutes it would be so.

## 97  HAST THOU COME TO THE END OF MY RESOURCES ?

His thoughts said, My enemies live and are mighty ; and yet I have required that they, even mine enemies, shall not triumph over me or over those whom Thou hast given me, my Father, for they are Thine. But I have come to the end of my resources.

His Father said, Hast thou come to the end of My resources? Is the Lord's hand shortened? Dost thou not know Him whom thou hast believed? Art thou not persuaded that He is able to keep that which thou hast committed unto Him? Know thy Lord and thy heart shall find repose in Him. Thine enemies shall not triumph over thee or over those whom I have given thee.

And the son said, I will cry unto God most high, unto God that performeth all things for me, even the cause that I have in hand. Lord, all my desire is before Thee.

## 8 UNPROFITABLE MOURNING

The son, while thinking of many whose day had been turned to night and who were trying to find light where no light was, read words about singing lustily with a good courage. And he wondered how he could sing lustily when he had neither courage nor lusty feelings because of the desolate.

Then he remembered an Indian proverb about fire-flies. They could not banish the night. And he knew that his wisdom lay not in unprofitable mourning over those who sit in darkness, but in taking a light better than fire-flies to any within reach.

## 99 A MIGHTY WORD

The son was reminded of a mighty word and a piercing: "Come, my people, enter thou into thy chambers, and shut thy doors about thee: hide thyself as it were for a little moment, until the indignation be overpast."

"Obey that word," said his Father, "Earnestly carry forth the light; but forget not to shut thy door."

## 100 THE LITTLE INCH OF THREAD

His thoughts said, What of people who never had a chance?

His Father said to him, Trust Me not to

disappoint thy trust.   Dost thou think that
the little inch of the thread of human life
which thou seest, is all that there is to see ?
Think of what thou knowest and hast
proved of My ways, and believe that what
thou dost not know is at least as loving as
what thou knowest and hast proved.


REFLECT ME

The son was grieved because some whom
he had hoped to help would not even look
at his Lord.   They were trying to satisfy
themselves with husks.   They were play-
ing with phantoms.

As he thought sorrowfully of those dear
to him, who were so near and yet so far, he
remembered how they and he together had
looked at the reflection of a mountain in
still water.   It was the reflection that first
caught their attention.   But presently they
had raised their eyes to the mountain.
Reflect Me, said his Father to him then.
They will look at thee.   Then they will
look up, and see Me.   And the stiller the
water the more perfect the reflection.

His thoughts said, I am distressed because of some very dear to me who have drifted away.

His Father said, They are dear to Me too. Mine is a following love. And when they return, My love will run to meet them.

His thoughts said, What of one who walked in the straight way of faith, but, being lured by the will-o'-the-wisp of false teaching, is wandering in the swamp ?

His Father said, I have stepping-stones in every swamp.

Then the son worshipped, saying, O Sovereign Lord, Thou Lover of souls, all the springs of my hope are in Thee. And like music played softly, melodious words sounded in his ears : *These things I have spoken unto you, that in Me ye might have peace.*

## 103 SHALL NOT THE HAND OF THE LORD BE FULLY SUFFICIENT ?

Sometimes for a while it was midnight for the son ; he could not see his way.

Then, just then, it often happened that a friend came to his house and he had nothing to set before him ; and Moses' anxious question was his, Shall sheep and oxen be slain for them, and shall it suffice them ? Or shall all the fish of the sea be gathered together, and shall it suffice them ?

But soon he remembered his Lord's gracious answer, Shall not the hand of the Lord be fully sufficient ?

And his Father said to him, Thou knowest the way to My house, thou canst find it even in the dark. So he went to his Father's house, and his Father gave him not three loaves only, but as many as he needed.

## 4 THE SEVERAL PEARLS

The son considered the bewildering truth that many things which helped his fellow-Christians did not help him. What was wrong, he wondered ; he himself, or what was offered for his help ?

This question perplexed him till he remembered that the wall of the City had twelve gates, and the twelve gates were twelve pearls. Every several gate was of one pearl. So there are many gates into the City, but each one is a pearl. And he knew that he must leave others to find their own gate, and be sure that he entered in by his own, for no other but his own would be a gate of pearl to him.

## 105 THE SEVEN LAMPS

The son came to see also that as the City with its twelve gates, so was that Tree of Light, the candlestick, with its seven lamps. Each lamp was like an almond flower, and each flower was a flower of light; but each was separate. And yet each almond flower was part of the candlestick of which it is written that it was one beaten work of pure gold.

The light may flow to him from one almond flower, to his brother from another. Not to judge the light of others, but to obey the light given to him was all that concerned him. Lord, what shall this man do ? What is that to thee ? Follow thou Me.

## THE WEARISOME GOODNESS OF THE GOOD

His thoughts said, I am ashamed to say it, but I find the goodness of some of the good very wearisome.

His Father said, It is not their goodness that wearieth thee, but the trappings and trimmings which they so often collect—those weary thee. True goodness is no more wearisome than the green of the Green Things of the earth. Try to ignore what will one day fall off and be forgotten. Try to see Me, thy Lord, in thy fellow-lovers. And consider, too, how wearisome thou must be to them, and yet, like thy patient angel, they bear with thee.


## FELLOWSHIP

His thoughts said, Jerusalem is built as a city that is compact together, that is at unity in itself, a city knit together whose fellowship is complete. We are, as it were, parts of one another, of one mind in an house, perfectly joined together in the same mind and in the same judgment.

Nothing less can content us. The thinnest film of separation is intolerable. But the attack on that position is persistent and violent. There is no end to it.

His Father said, Nor ever will be. Measure the preciousness of Spiritual Unity by the persistence and the violence of Satanic attack.

The son said, Some say that the standard of love is set too high. Do little ruffles matter ? they say ; there are sure to be some among fellow-workers.

His Father said, Ask them to go with thee to Calvary and think that thought there—if they can.

## 108 AND PREPARETH A WAY

After a time of contrary winds and much toil in rowing, He whose name is Wonderful did wondrously, and there was a great calm.

Then the son said, Blessed be the Lord God who spoke with His mouth and hath with His hand fulfilled it. There hath not failed one word of all His good promises. Not one thing hath failed thereof.

And his Father said, Whoso offereth the sacrifice of thanksgiving glorifieth Me ; and prepareth a way that I may shew him the salvation of God.

## 9 THEN LOOK UP

The son thought of one who had a vision of voices, a noise, thunders, earthquakes and tumult. And behold, two great serpents came forth, both ready for conflict ; and there came from them a great voice. Surely it is so now, said the son. And in many lands hast Thou not delivered Thy strength unto captivity, Thy glory into the enemy's hand ? And though he knew that all had been foreseen and foretold, yet he was grieved and burdened ; and he said, They have scoffed at the tardiness of Thy Messiah's footsteps.

Then the Comforter led him to these words : And when these things begin to come to pass, then look up, and lift up your heads ; for your redemption draweth nigh.

His thoughts said, The hate in the world is like a horror of great darkness.

His Father said, Love, not hate, is eternal. Love, not hate, was set up from everlasting, from the beginning, or ever the earth was. When there were no depths, Love was brought forth ; when there were no fountains abounding with water. Before the mountains were settled, before the hills was Love brought forth. When I appointed the foundations of the earth, then Love was by Me, as One brought up with Me : and Love was daily My delight, rejoicing always before Me, rejoicing in My habitable earth. That which was at the beginning, that alone abideth. The woe and grief and cruelty of man to man— these are of time. Love is of Eternity. Disbelieve this and thy heart will break. Believe it and thou canst endure.

## 111 PAIN OF CHILDREN, ANIMALS ?

His thoughts said, Why was the world created ? The adversary hath spread out his hands upon all her pleasant things. The wickedness of the wicked doth not cease. The pages of history are scarlet with the suffering of the innocent. O poor world! what of the pain of children? what of the pain of animals? That "not a moth with vain desire is shrivelled in a fruitless fire or but subserves another's gain" is no consolation. What is the gain to the moth? Miserable comforters are ye all who offer this chaff for wheat.

His Father said, It is written, "The tender mercies of the Lord are over all His works." All, not some. Trust their Creator to justify those words. Let His words be true and thy faithless fears be liars.

## NOT AT . . . BUT AT . . .

The son prayed, Be not far from me, for trouble is near, and his thoughts said, How can one be glad or even peaceful when trouble is near?

His Father said, Before thy Saviour went to Bethany, when trouble was near, He was peaceful ; and He said to His disciples, I am glad. For He looked not at the things that are seen, but at the things which are not seen. Canst thou not do likewise ?

Look through the approaching trouble, whatever it be, to that which is beyond it. Then thou wilt find that thou canst be peaceful, and even be able to say, " I am glad." For the Lord sitteth above the water-flood and the Lord remaineth a King for ever. The Lord shall give strength unto His people : the Lord shall give His people the blessing of peace.

## 113 THERE IS A PLACE BY ME

His thoughts said, Before me continually is the grief of wounds, confusion, suspense, distress.

His Father said, Behold, there is a place by Me, and thou shalt stand upon a rock. Then, as a frightened child on a storm-swept mountain-side would gratefully take his father's hand, and stand on a rock in a place by him, fearing no evil—so it was with the son. For he knew that though the earth be removed and the waters be carried into the midst of the sea, that rock by his Father would never be moved. And he remembered words about things that can be shaken and things that will remain. And though no small tempest lay on him, he said to the multitude of thoughts whose voices sought to disturb him, Sirs, be of good cheer ; for I believe God that it shall be even as it was told me. For as His majesty is, so also is His mercy.

## 4 FRET NOT THYSELF BECAUSE OF——

The son knew some who had trusted that they would be delivered from the hand of an evil man, but they had not been delivered : the evil man had brought his wicked devices to pass and he was prospering in his way. Then the son remembered the command which ran down to the roots of life and was exceedingly difficult to obey : " Fret not thyself because of the man who bringeth wicked devices to pass." And he thought of another word that dealt with burning injuries : "Vengeance is Mine ; I will repay, saith the Lord." And he saw that by fretting he could not help his friends. It tended only to evil doing ; for it kindled a fire in him that was not a holy fire ; and it made him the less able to do anything for them.

So he learned to turn the spiritual energy which he had spent in fretting, into prayer for them. And as he did so, he knew that now at last he was helping his friends.

## 115 GO TO CALVARY

Then to that son the question came. Dost thou know the way to Calvary ? And following that way he saw Pilate, after he had scourged the Lord Jesus, deliver Him to be crucified. He saw the soldiers take his Lord into the common hall, and gather unto Him the whole band of soldiers. And they stripped Him, and put on Him a scarlet robe. And when they had platted a crown of thorns, they put it upon His head, and a reed in His right hand ; And they bowed the knee before Him, and mocked Him, And they spit upon Him, and took the reed, and smote Him on the head, and led Him away to crucify Him. And they crucified Him.

"In all times of thy tribulation over the triumph of evil," said the Father, "go to Calvary."

## THE FOUR ANGELS OF THE FOUR CORNERS

The son grieved because of many little unprotected things, as well as because of the great and noble who were lashed by bitter winds. He found solace in the vision of the four angels who stand on the four corners of the earth. No smallest leaf on any tree may be shaken by the wind till the word is given by the angel who ascendeth from the East, having the seal of the living God. But the evil one tried to distress him by saying, It is folly to stay thy heart upon a vision of the future. So the son found a declaration of his God made long ago ; and on that rock he stood:

Now for the comfortless troubles' sake of the needy : and because of the deep sighing of the poor, I will up, saith the Lord : and will help every one from him that swelleth against him, and will set him at nought.

## 117 THE END WILL EXPLAIN ALL THINGS

His thoughts said, What of the two witnesses to whom was given power to shut heaven, and over waters and to smite the earth ? Even they, Thy faithful ones, were overcome when the beast that ascendeth out of the bottomless pit made war against them.

His Father said, After three days and a half the Spirit of Life from God entered into them and they stood upon their feet ; and great fear fell upon them which saw them. And they heard a great Voice from heaven saying unto them, Come up hither. And they ascended up to heaven in a cloud ; and their enemies beheld them.

Beware lest thou stay thy thoughts at the beginning of My dealings with any nation or with any soul. The end will explain all things. Till then, great peace have they which love My Law and nothing shall offend them.

## AT THE END OF THE DAYS

His thoughts found relief in a torrent of prayer, Righteous art Thou, O Lord, when I plead with Thee : yet let me talk with Thee of Thy judgments : Wherefore doth the way of the wicked prosper ? Up, Lord, disappoint him, cast him down. Break Thou the power of the ungodly and malicious ; take away his ungodliness. O let the wickedness of the wicked come to an end. Make their faces ashamed, O Lord, that they may seek Thy name. O let the sorrowful sighing of the prisoners come before Thee. Thou seest the oppression that is done upon the earth ; Lord, how long wilt Thou look upon this ?

His Father said, Dost thou think that it hath not grieved Me at My heart ? But

87

there is an end. Thou hast not seen to the end. At the end of the days thou shalt understand.

## 119 IT IS MINE OWN INFIRMITY

The thoughts of the son said, The end is far away and trouble is near. And he found himself akin to one who, long ago, had communed with his heart and searched out his spirits ; and he said, Will the Lord absent Himself for ever ? and will He be no more intreated ? Is His mercy clean gone for ever ? and is His promise come utterly to an end for evermore ? Hath God forgotten to be gracious ? and will He shut up His loving kindness in displeasure ?

Then he was quiet for a while as braver words flowed over him. And he said, It is mine own infirmity : but I will remember the years of the right hand of the most Highest.

# THERE SHALL BE AN END

But still the son felt like a long shore on which all the waves of pain of all the world were beating.

His Father drew near to him and said, There is only one shore long enough for that. Upon My love, that long, long shore, those waves are beating now ; but thou canst have fellowship with Me. And I promise thee that there shall be an end ; and all tears shall be wiped from off all faces.

# THE SCALES

The son saw a pair of scales. In the one scale was sorrow. In the other was joy. Sometimes the scales hung even. Sometimes one out-weighed the other. But as he watched he saw a change pass over the sorrow ; it was turned into joy and poured into the scale of joy. And he understood the words, "I have more than an over-weight of joy for all the affliction which has befallen me." For he saw his travails, tears, watchings, strivings increase by just so much the more his shining heap of happiness. With awe and with wonder he also saw that each experience of distress had put into his hand a golden key called Comfort. And as he used this key the innermost rooms of troubled hearts opened to the Comforter. Then the son rejoiced as he thought of the Man of Sorrows, Christ Crucified. How much more surely will His sorrow be turned into joy when the pleasure of the Lord shall prosper in His hand, and He shall see of the travail of His soul and shall be satisfied.

## 122 WITH DESIRE I HAVE DESIRED

Everything in the son felt with him who said, I am not worthy that Thou shouldest come under my roof, and yet he said, O when wilt Thou come unto me? I will walk within my house with a perfect heart ; for I know that Thy commandment is life everlasting. As his thoughts were occupied thus, he found himself on the shore of the sea. And he took a grain of sand from the miles of sand about him and he held it in his hand.  Then he knew that his desire for the Presence of his Lord was like a little grain for smallness in comparison with his Lord's desire to come under his roof, for that was like the measure of the measureless sands.  And as his thoughts followed this great thought, Jesus his Lord answered and said unto him, With desire I have desired.

## HIS FATHER PROMISED

The son said to his Father, Father, wilt Thou strengthen me to live through this day ?  His Father promised to strengthen him and took his fears away.  The son asked for peace ;  his Father promised to garrison his heart with peace.  The son asked that he might rejoice in his Lord, whatever happened to distress him.  And his Father promised that too.  Then the son asked that nothing should come between him and his Lord.  And he was persuaded that neither things present, nor things to come shall be able to separate him from the love of God, which is in Christ Jesus our Lord.

The son said, I should be stedfast and victorious ; but the house of my soul is not always so with Thee.

His Father said, Though thy house be not always so with Me, yet I have made with thee an everlasting covenant, ordered in all things and sure. Though thy feelings may be changeful as the changeful form of clouds on a windy day, yet I, thy God, am stedfast for ever.

And with a quickened gratitude the son said, Thou, O God, sentest a gracious rain upon Thine inheritance and refreshedst it when it was weary.

## 125 PICTURES

The thoughts of the son ran thus : My hopes painted beautiful pictures, but they are fading one by one.

Then his Father spoke to him : Thy hopes painted pictures ? Destroy all those pictures. To watch them slowly fading is weakening to the soul. Dare then to destroy them. Thou canst if thou wilt.

Thou must if thou wouldest be My warrior-son. I will give thee other pictures instead of those thy hopes painted. Look up, O thou son of My love.

Then the son looked up, and he saw a Cross raised high against the sunlight, then a darkness that might be felt. And he heard, as it were, an echo of a voice, "Father, glorify Thy name"; and a Voice that answered, "I have both glorified it and will glorify it again." And he knew that strength and beauty were in the Sanctuary and would presently pour forth. Calvary was not the end of that day's story. And his heart stayed itself upon this assurance : He shall choose our inheritance for us—no fading picture that, but the excellency of Jacob whom He loved.

## BETTER THAN AT THY BEGINNINGS

The son said, Forgive me, my Father, but sometimes I wonder if even in the Other Life there will be that for which my heart longeth.

His Father said, In My Presence is fulness of joy ; can fulness be less than full ? At My right hand there are pleasures for evermore ; can pleasures be less than delight ? Dear child of My love, trust My love, Would I leave one longing unsatisfied ? Thou dost not know thy Father if thou thinkest that I would. Thou shalt be satisfied with the plenteousness of My House ; I will give thee to drink of My pleasures as out of a river. Dost thou think that nothing could ever be as beautiful as once it was ? Turn thine eyes from thy beautiful beginnings—I will do better unto thee than at thy beginnings.

## 127 LOVE IS FIRE

The Father said to the son, Tell Me, My child, thy heart's desire.

The son said, My heart's desire is to be like my Lord, who, having loved His own, loved them unto the end.

The Father said, But love is fire, consuming fire. Dost thou ask for fire ?

The son thought of some who had not

shrunk back from fire. Their way had become a fiery way. Few would understand ; many would blame as they walked in that way. It looked an impossible way. But his Father was surprised that he used so faithless a word : Am I not the God of the Impossible ? Dare to believe for the Impossible. Very soon it will be said, They walked in the midst of the stones of fire more than conquerors. They sang as it were a new song.

## WAIT THY TO-MORROW

The son thought of a hope that had utterly perished. It was as withered grass. As he thought of it he seemed to see an old man climbing a mountain. His eyes were not dimmed, but they were wistful. His hope had utterly perished. It was as withered grass.

For the Lord had said unto Moses, Behold thou shalt sleep with thy fathers. And Moses went up from the plains unto the mountain. And the Lord shewed him the land where he fain would be ; and He said, I have caused thee to see it with thine eyes, but thou shalt not go over thither. So Moses the servant of the Lord died there.

Then the son saw a page turned in the Book of Eternity, and the man was in the land where he had hoped to be. Of the myriads in Paradise he and one other were chosen to meet their Lord in that land. And behold there talked with Him two men, which were Moses and Elijah ; who appeared in glory, and spake of His departure which He was about to accomplish at Jerusalem.

" If thou couldest ask him," said a voice in the ear of the son, " whether, had the choice been given, he would have chosen to be there on that earlier day, or with his Lord on this later day, what dost thou think he would say ? "

And the son knew.

Then the Voice that was dearest of all voices to the son spoke to him in words not to be repeated, for they were for him alone ; but he knew that always the Father holdeth in loving remembrance that which the child in grief called withered. And what Love holdeth, Love quickeneth. And what Love withdraweth, Love multiplieth. The child shall meet his perished hope in bud and blossom to-morrow. And his Father said, Wait thy to-morrow, My child.


## BY HIS CROSS AND PASSION

The son felt sometimes that human words soared too high for his human heart to follow. And sometimes they skimmed with too light an air over depths which were very deep. But he found himself at home in the Psalms, and he walked up and down there as one who was at home.

And the Psalms led him to Him who was poured out like water, and Him he followed as He trod the common roads of life, till at last he was with Him under some olive trees on a hillside, and then on a hill outside a city gate.

Now in the place where He was crucified there was a garden. To this garden the son went in the moonlight before dawn, and there his Master met him and called him by his name. So by His Cross and Passion the son was brought into the glory of His Resurrection. And with one who had lost sight of Him for a while, he fell at His feet, saying, My Lord and my God.

## 130 ART THOU WILLING ?

The Father said, Art thou willing to be crucified ?

The son answered, By Thy grace I am willing.

His Father said, Art thou willing to let thy Lord choose thy Cross and the nails that shall pierce thy hands and thy feet ?

The son answered, My Lord shall choose what He will.

His Father said, Art thou willing that thy house on earth may be a little emptier so that My House may be the fuller ?

The son was silent for a while, at last he answered, I am willing.

Then the Father loved the son very dearly.

His thoughts said, I do not understand
how such gladness as this that is given can
be when nothing that I expected is happen-
ing, and much that I hoped would never
happen has been allowed to come.

For a while his Father was silent in His
love, and the son was silent too. At last
he thought he heard these words : It is
written of thy dear Lord, " Thy God hath
anointed Thee with the Oil of Gladness."
With a little of that blessed Oil He hath
anointed even thee. And then—and this
was a word of wonder to the son—his
Father said clearly, *I thank thee for thy
joy.*

## 2 MY SAPPHIRES

The son remembered those who out of
weakness were made strong and yet had
never seen the walls of Jericho fall down.
They had suffered the violence of fire ;
the fire was not quenched for them. They
did not escape the edge of the sword ;
the sword was sharpened for them. They

did not receive their dead raised to life. They did not obtain the promises.

His Father said, These all died in faith, not having received the promises. But they saw them afar off, were persuaded of them, and embraced them. Theirs was the blessing of the Unoffended. I could trust them with the Unexplained. Dost thou not know any such to-day? If thou dost, watch carefully and thou shalt see them strengthened to abide the proof. They will not change their colour when the light is dim.

Then the son remembered reading of a sapphire whose colour was so pure that, unlike the ordinary kind, it retained its blue, a heavenly blue, even by candle-light.

And his Father said, These of whom I have told thee are My Sapphires.


133 BE COMFORTED ABOUT THY FRIEND

The son had a companion in tribulation, and in the Kingdom and patience of

Jesus Christ. To this friend some went who multiplied words without knowledge, and they heaped them upon him till he was crushed under their weight ; and his joy was like a tree cut down.

When the son took this matter to his Father, his Father said, I have many foolish children who darken counsel. They even try to make My words the frame of their opinions. But he who dwelleth in the Secret Place is not long disquieted. Though at first he be overwhelmed, he shall soon learn to say to his soul, "Wherefore hearest thou men's words ? It is a very small thing that I should be judged of man's judgment. He that judgeth me is the Lord." And though for a little while his joy be like a tree cut down, it will sprout again, and through the scent of water it will bud, and bring forth boughs like a plant. For he is like a tree planted by the rivers of water. Be comforted about thy friend.

His thoughts said, Some are poor and weak and ill, and they are not kindly tended. I know of others who are at the end of their patience.

His Father said, They are My nurslings. And He brought to his mind many tender words : '' The Lord thy God will bear thee as a nursling ; His left hand is under my head, and His right hand doth embrace me ; He comforteth them that are losing patience.'' No circumstances could be too difficult for Him. He was nearer to the ill than even the limitations and distresses of illness. These like iron rings encircled them. He was within the innermost of those iron rings.

And the son took refuge in the prayer, Do Thou for them, O God the Lord.

## 135 A FENCE OF FEATHERS

The son felt fenced in.

His Father took him to the fence and bid him look ; he looked and he did not see a

hedge of thorn or a barbed wire entangle-
ment ; he saw a fence of feathers : " With
His feathers shall He make a fence for
thee."

## 6 I WILL PUT UP WITH THEE

The son feared lest those who were fenced
in with him might weary, and he said,
How can they put up with me ?

His Father brought to his mind an
ancient promise, " *I will put up with thee*,"
and He said, I am with them that uphold
thy soul ; therefore they will not weary.
As for Me, My word is pledged : I will not
fail thee, nor forsake thee, until thou hast
finished all the work for the service of the
house of the Lord. And I will not fail
thee nor forsake thee then.

## 37 WEARIED WITH HIS JOURNEY

His thoughts said, I could do better work
for my Lord if it were not that I am tired.
I am tired of being tired.

His Father said, Jesus, being wearied

with His journey, sat thus on the well.
Art thou not willing to be wearied with thy
journey ?  Many are wearied in the service
of self, the world, earthly glory—thou art
loosed from that bondage.  Rejoice in thy
liberty to be weary for His sake who loved
thee and gave Himself for thee.  Abide in
His love, and thou shalt learn to give as He
gave, even in weariness ;  to live as He
lived, more than conqueror over the flesh.

## 138  IN A BODY THAT I PREPARED

His thoughts said, O that God would grant
me the thing that I long for, even a quick
release.  Yea, I would exult in pain that
spareth not but breaketh the vessel in
pieces as a potter's vessel is broken.  I
would exult in that which set me free to
serve in vigour again.

His Father said, My holy Child Jesus
spoke differently.  His only care was to
fulfil My will.  He said, "I am content
to do it."  He did not ask for a quick
release.  Listen to Him : "I have glorified Thee on the earth : I have finished the

work which Thou gavest Me to do." Hast thou finished the work that I have given thee to do ?

But the son said, Surely the corruptible body presseth down the soul ; the earthly tabernacle weigheth down the mind ? And his Father answered, When He, thy Master and Lord, came into the world, He said, " A body hast Thou prepared Me." In that body He did My Will. As He was, so art thou, in a body that I prepared.

## BESIDE THE THINGS WHICH I OMIT

His thoughts said, There is something very noble in St. Paul's list of sufferings, labours, stripes, prisons, persecutions. They are glorious sufferings. Nothing that I have to bear could find a place in such a list.

His Father said, Hast thou read the words, *Beside the things which I omit, Beside the things that come out of course?* What if the things that thou hast to bear be those that come out of course, the omitted things of that list ?

His thoughts said, The things which have happened unto me do not seem to have fallen out unto the furtherance of the Gospel —they seem to be very hindering.

His Father said, If thou hadst understanding in the visions of God, thou wouldest know that all things work together for good not only for him who loveth, but for that on which his heart is set. And to the words, "all things," there are no exceptions.

## 141 I WILL SPEAK PRIVATELY TO THAT HEART

The son said, But if one, whom in other days Thou didst often touch and heal, be ill even after pressing through to Thee with full purpose of heart, what then?

His Father said, Then I will speak privately to his heart. The world will not hear what I say, but his heart will hear. The word will be fulfilled to him, By day the Lord will command His mercy, and manifest it by night.

## NOT I, PAUL, THE PRISONER OF NERO

His thoughts said, And yet—frustrations, limitations, O to have done with them !

His Father said, Remember, *I, Paul, the prisoner of Christ Jesus; not I, Paul, the prisoner of Nero.*

And the son called to mind a pearl-oyster shell which had surprised and charmed him. Two friends looking at it together saw it differently. One saw a broad black band running round the rim. The other saw a rainbow. Yet both were looking at the same time at the same shell. And he knew that what he saw depended upon how he looked, and how the light fell upon that on which he looked. He was in Nero's prison, but he was not the prisoner of Nero. He was the prisoner of Christ Jesus, his triumphant, adorable Lord.

## AS THOU HAST BORNE THOU SHALT ALSO BEAR

His thoughts said, Some words baffle me. How can our body of humiliation be fashioned like unto the glorious body of our Lord ?

His Father said, Canst thou explain the words, " According to the working whereby He is able even to subdue all things unto Himself " ?   If thou hast no line to sound the depths of that " according to ", why be surprised that thou art baffled by any other words ?

The son answered, I know that Thou canst do everything, but all in me beareth the image of the earthy.   Then he listened in silence awhile, and he thought he heard a Voice saying, As thou hast borne the image of the earthy, thou shalt also bear the image of the heavenly.

144 A GARDEN OF DELIGHT

His thoughts said, Life used to be to me a Garden of Delight, for I could minister continually as every day's work required ; but now it is not so.

His Father said, It is written that some were expressed by name to give thanks to the Lord.   Sing songs to Him and sing hymns to Him. The hearts that seek His pleasure shall rejoice. Seek the Lord and be strong—thou hast read those happy words. If thou art one of that company, expressed by name, is it not enough to cause any kind of life to be a Garden of Delight ?

## ONLY FOR A SEASON

His thoughts said, There is so much to help me, and I have so many comforts that I am ashamed to feel oppressed. And yet at times I am, as it were, bound down by oppressions.

His Father said, Take a very simple prayer and say it now : Lord, I am oppressed, undertake for me, ease me. This oppression is only for a season. Is there not heart's ease in that ?

The son answered, Thy consolations have soothed my soul. Thou hast loosed my bonds. And he remembered the story of Joseph, who was laid in iron—*until* the King sent and loosed him and let him go free. And he knew that there was an end to bonds and rejoiced in the words, The Lord looseth the fettered ones.

## 146 THE SUM OF THINGS SHOWN ABOUT BONDS

If illness and pain were from God, doctors and nurses would be working against Him, not with Him. Luke the beloved Physician would be Luke the mistaken Physician. And no loyal child of the Father, crushed by accident or illness, could touch the slightest alleviation, not even a hot-water bottle ; for to resist would be rebellion. But if an enemy hath done this, the Christian has a good right to resist. We are not told why the enemy is allowed to do as he does in this or any other realm of life. Deut. 28. 29 reminds us that God has His secret things. His way is in the sea and His path in the great waters and His footsteps are not known.

The oil of James and the figs of Hezekiah's poultice, those ancient Eastern remedies, are with us to-day in the form of countless healing helps. They are God's good gift to us. Sometimes He heals His own by a Touch which thrills the whole being. The recovered one is like Peter's wife's mother then. There is no convalescence. Life's duty is taken up straightway. Sometimes he heals through what we call means. Either way it is He who heals, and it is for Him to choose how He will heal. Our part is to co-operate, to set the forces of the will toward health, and to refuse to be dominated by the feeling of illness, depression, selfishness, weariness. If that be done, the prayer of faith is answered. The sick one is made sound so that he himself is well. (We are not our bodies.)

### 2.

And if, after all, bodily healing does not come, as little as may be of the disappointment should be shown to others. They have their own burdens to bear ; why add to them ? Strength will be given to accept the answer of 2 Cor. 12. 9 and Luke 7. 23, without yielding to weakening reactions. And perhaps, very, very humbly the ill one may follow into the deep places opened in Col. 1. 24 and John 11. 4. ("There was some mysterious sense in which the sick man suffered in behalf of God's glory, and was not merely a passive instrument.") Then looking up to his Father, believing that the day, even this kind of day, continues by His arrangement, as the Septuagint of Ps. 119. 91 has it, he learns to trust that the day so arranged will not be lived in vain. This is no easy acquiescence. There is nothing easy about it. But the first answer to the prayer of Phil. 4. 6 is peace. The first answer to the prayer of faith is peace. And to peace is added fortitude ; and to fortitude longsuffering with joyfulness.

### 3.

This joyfulness can be sharply assaulted, for to yield to bodily ills at all feels unsoldierly.

At such times the will must resolutely turn from that aspect of illness which words, like infirm, invalid, disabled, laid aside, imply. We need be none of these feeble things. We can be firm, valid and able for some things, if not for others ; and the Captain of our salvation does not treat His wounded soldiers as a housekeeper does her cracked china : He never " shelves " us. The singers sang, and the trumpeters sounded : and all this continued until the burnt offering was finished, is a bugle call for a difficult day.

For we are still soldiers ; we enlisted for life. And soldiers have a sword. In the twelfth century, so tradition says, a sword was fashioned from a fragment of a meteorite. It is as perfect to-day as it was the day it left the hands of the armourer. Not a stain of rust is found on that blade to which the Arabs have given the name, the Sword of God, the Life-endowed.

Our Sword is like that, stainless as Eternity. The accidents of time cannot affect it. It is ours for use in the wars of the Lord. The only thing that matters, then, is to throw all the energies of our being into the faithful use of this precious blade, and to refuse to scatter thoughts or sympathies on the trifles of the flesh which we are tempted to magnify. They cannot weaken the effectual action of the weapon that is ours as truly now as ever it was—The Sword of God, the Life-endowed, the Sword of the Spirit, which is the word of God.

### 4.

So we come back to this : we may be in Nero's prison, but we are not Nero's prisoners. "My soul is among lions" appears to be true at times. "I was delivered out of the mouth of the lion" is a delightful word for a delightful experience —it was once St. Paul's. But if we are trusted with disappointment, as he was, and we find ourselves again among lions (re-arrested, and in bonds), the word still holds true, *I, Paul, the prisoner of Christ Jesus*. Never does Paul attempt to explain the paradox, any more than he explained why he left Trophimus at Miletus sick—a friend for whom he had surely prayed the prayer of faith. Explanations belong to Another Day.

Till that day dawn, though we may be in Nero's prison, our prison-cell may be an illuminated place. " And a light shined in the cell "—these are shining words. They are singing words :

> *And a light shined in the cell,*
> *And there was not any wall,*
> *And there was no dark at all,*
> *Only Thou, Emmanuel.*
>
> *Light of Love shined in the cell,*
> *Turned to gold the iron bars,*
> *Opened windows to the stars,*
> *Peace stood there as sentinel.*
>
> *Dearest Lord, how can it be*
> *That Thou art so kind to me?*
> *Love is shining in my cell,*
> *Jesus, my Emmanuel.*

# 7 HOW GREAT IS HIS GOODNESS AND HOW GREAT IS HIS BEAUTY

The son remembered that Job was led into the place of peace, not by an explanation of the mystery of suffering, or even of the mysteries of creation, for nothing was explained ; but by hearing the Voice of his Creator and Redeemer, and by knowing that He was mindful of him.

And he thought of the countless touches of tenderness upon his life, and remembering these, he worshipped saying, How great is His goodness, and how great is His beauty !

## 148 ONE DAY THOU SHALT SEE

The son was in deep sorrow, and he said, Never, never did I think of not being with him who is my very heart, when he came to the brink of the river.

His Father said, Will he miss thy hand whom My hand holdeth ?

But his soul refused comfort and he said, What if he falter in the lonely places his feet must tread ?

His Father answered gently, Hast thou forgotten the Powers of Calvary ? They overcame by the Blood of the Lamb. Hold fast to the faithfulness of My eternal word. However overcome the poor flesh may appear to be, the spirit even now is overcoming. One day thou shalt see all that is hidden from thee now.

## 9 WATER OF THE WELL OF BETHLEHEM

But, still uncomforted, the son cried out, O that one would give me to drink of the water of the well of Bethlehem, which is by the gate !

His Father said, And if at this moment thy heart's desire were given to thee, what wouldest thou do ? Wouldest thou not pour it out unto thy Lord ? Do so with the longing for that which is as the water of the well of Bethlehem to thee. Pour out the desire of thine heart to Me now. I will gather it up and give it to thee another day.

## 0 AND THE STRENGTH COMMANDED CAME

The love of the Father was life to the son, and yet his thoughts said, It is as if something had given way. The walls of my being are shaken. There is nothing in me but brokenness.

His Father said, Thou shalt not break. Behold I have painted thy walls on My hands, and thou art continually before Me. Thy God hath sent forth strength for thee. Thy God hath commanded thy strength.

Then the son, remembering that, because the words of his Lord were spirit and life, they were able to convey that of which they spoke, did at last gratefully receive those words. And the strength commanded came.

## 151 THAT RIVER LEAST OF ALL

His thoughts said, Is the love of a dearly loved one the same after the river is crossed, or is it so swallowed up in joy that it is a little different ?

His Father said, It is not swallowed up in joy. It is the same love, different only in that it increaseth for ever with the increase of God. Of that thou canst know nothing yet. It is very far beyond thee. But this is within thy grasp : Many waters cannot quench love, neither can the floods drown it—Rivers shall not drown it, *that* river least of all.

## 2 BEING THE CHILDREN OF THE RESURRECTION

His thoughts said, O to see what he is doing !

His Father said, He is walking in the Land of the Living. He is singing in the Courts of My House. He is serving in the fulness of joy, and rejoicing in the fulness of strength. He is serving without the distraction of the flesh in the freedom of the beauty of holiness. He has seen Him whom his soul loveth. He is satisfied. Take comfort from this : all the pain is on thy side, all the joy is on his. He will never feel the pang that rendeth thee. And then like great music came these words :

Neither can they die any more:
For they are equal unto the angels;
And are the Children of God,
Being the Children of the Resurrection.

## 153 THOU SHALT LEARN TO DO WITHOUT

The son answered his Father, saying, The Lord hath heard the voice of my weeping, I am well pleased that the Lord hath heard the voice of my prayer. Right dear in the sight of the Lord is the death of His saints. Thou Thyself hast led him over death to the Singing Land. And I know that there is a joy of birds in that land, and as for those who dwell there, joy shall take possession of them, and on their head shall be praise and exultation. Therefore I will offer to Thee the sacrifice of thanksgiving. Blessed be the Lord God of Israel from everlasting to everlasting.

And now, said his Father tenderly, thou shalt learn the lesson set to the weaned child. Thou shalt learn to do without.


## 154 I AM THE GOD OF THE STARS

There was a night when the son was greatly distressed. He saw those he loved, beset, because they were bereft of one on whom he had counted to be a help to them. What if they lost their way? He had turned out the light, and there was no moon; but suddenly, between the branches of a leafy tree that grew outside his window, he saw the stars. At first he saw them distant, cold, and unregarding. They had looked down through countless generations upon broken hearts. They meant nothing to him, till suddenly piercing through the pain of the hour came words, simple as the words one would speak to a sorrowful child:

*I am the God of the stars.*
*They do not lose their way,*
*Not one do I mislay,*
*Their times are in My hand,*
*They move at my command.*

*I am the God of the stars.*
*To-day as yesterday*
*The God of thee and thine,*
*Who are less thine than Mine;*
*And shall Mine go astray?*

*I am the God of the stars.*
*Lift up thine eyes and see*
*As far as mortal may*
*Into Eternity;*
*And rest thy heart on Me.*

The son looked again, and now the stars were not distant, cold, unregarding. And he looked unto the God of the stars from whom cometh our help.

## 155 UNTO MYSELF

The son asked, What is death ?

His Saviour answered, I will come again and receive you unto Myself ; that where I am, there ye may be also.

The son repeated those peaceful words, *I will receive you unto Myself* . . . And he wondered that men had given so harsh a name to anything so gentle as that which those words signified. They seemed melodious to him, each word like the pure note of a bell. And they were, he thought, as full of life as a flower in the sunshine is full of light.

## 156 WHAT DO WE MEAN BY HEAVEN ?

To one who said, We speak of Heaven, what do we mean by Heaven ? the son answered, as turning to Another,

Heaven is to behold Thy face in righteousness ;

To be satisfied when I awake with Thy likeness ;

To adore Thee in purity of spirit ;

To serve like Thy ministers, who do Thy pleasure ;

To know that even I shall never more grieve Thee ;

To exult in Thy Crowning, O my Saviour, my Redeemer ;

To be with Thee for ever who hast long been my Desire ;

To be with my beloved ones and never more be parted ;

To see all the comfortless comforted and all wrongs righted ;

To have light and leisure to learn, and infinite power to love.

If this be not Heaven, what is Heaven ?


## TO WHICH WORD ?

Near the end of the day the son looked back. Among all the Comfortable words which had been spoken to him, to which did he now turn most often ? And he knew it was to this : The Blood of Jesus Christ His Son cleanseth us from all sin ; and this: Beloved, now are we the sons of God, and it doth not yet appear what we shall be : but we know that when He shall appear, we shall be like Him ; for we shall see Him as He is.

## 158 THE PRAYER OF THE SON

*Think through me, Thoughts of God,*
  *My father, quiet me,*
*Till in Thy holy presence, hushed,*
  *I think Thy thoughts with Thee.*

*Think through me, Thoughts of God,*
  *That always, everywhere,*
*The stream that through my being flows*
  *May homeward pass in prayer.*

*Think through me, Thoughts of God,*
  *And let my own thoughts be*
*Lost like the sand-pools on the shore*
  *Of the eternal sea.*

# NOTE

SOME familiar Scriptures are quoted in the less familiar rendering of the Septuagint, so that another facet of the jewel may be shown.

5. 2 Chron. 20. 20.
23. Zeph. 3. 17.
25. Deut. 12. 7.
59. Num. 11. 23.
60. Deut. 1. 30.
61. 2 Chron. 20. 17 ; Ps. 40. 17.
134 Deut. 1. 31.
136. Isa. 46. 4.
141. Ps. 42. 8.

The " fence of feathers," is from Kay, Ps. 91. 4.
" He comforteth them that are losing patience," is from Ecclesiasticus 17. 24.

# SOME DOHNAVUR BOOKS

*Amy Carmichael of Dohnavur*, by Frank Houghton (cloth)

**by Amy Carmichael**
*Gold Cord*. The Story of the Fellowship (cloth)

STORIES OF INDIAN WOMEN
*Ponnammal* (paper)
*Mimosa* (cloth)
*Ploughed Under* (cloth)
*Kohila* (paper)

DEVOTIONAL BOOKS
*His Thoughts Said . . . His Father Said . . .* (cloth and paper)
*Edges of His Ways* (cloth)
*If* (cloth and paper)
*God's Missionary* (paper)
*Rose from Brier* (cloth)
*Gold by Moonlight* (cloth)
*Figures of the True* (paper)

BOOKS OF VERSE
*Toward Jerusalem* (paper)
*Wings*. Words and music (cloth and paper)

**Printed** in Great Britain by Fletcher & Son Ltd, Norwich